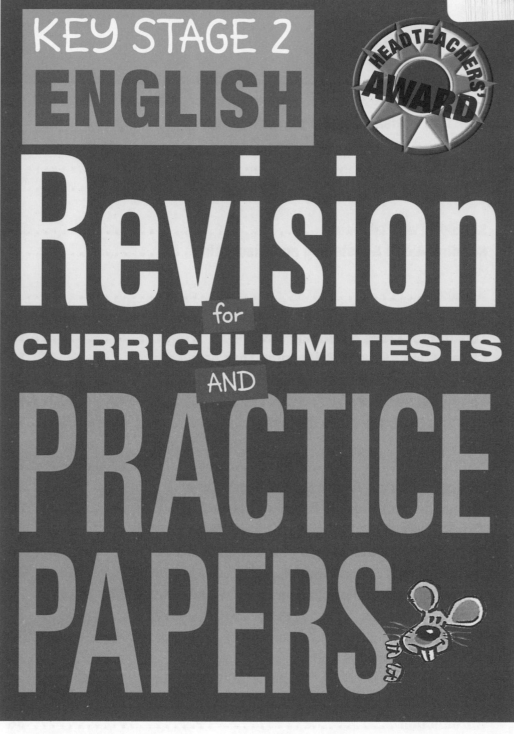

KEY STAGE 2
ENGLISH

Revision
for
CURRICULUM TESTS
AND
PRACTICE PAPERS

Author
Camilla de la Bédoyère

Consultant Editor
Christine Warwick

This is a Flame Tree Book
First published in 2002

07 08 09 10 11

10 9 8 7 6 5 4 3

ISBN 1-903817-68-4

Flame Tree is part of
The Foundry Creative Media Company Ltd
Crabtree Hall, Crabtree Lane, Fulham,
London SW6 6TY

Visit our website: www.flametreepublishing.com

Copyright © The Foundry 2007

Thanks to Jenny Bishop, Lucy Bradbury, Michelle Clare,
Vicky Garrard, Chris Herbert, Julia Rolf, Colin Rudderham,
Graham Stride, Nick Wells, Polly Willis and Tom Worsley.

A copy of the CIP data for this book is available from the
British Library

Printed in China

Photographs courtesy of Topham Picturepoint

Contents

Foreword

In today's ever-changing educational climate in which targets, levels of achievement and school league-tables grab headline news, it is important to remember what is at the core of it all: the education of your child.

Children learn at different speeds and achieve different levels during their early years at school, so it is important that a child is encouraged to work to the best of his or her ability, whatever their standard.

The Head Teacher's Awards, which many schools use, is a simple, yet highly effective way to motivate children. In the classroom a child may be given an HTA for a particularly good piece of work, or for trying hard in a subject they struggle with, or for neat handwriting, fluent reading, or imaginative creative writing. The list is endless, yet the effect of the HTA on the child is great: they feel valued and that something they have really tried hard at has been noticed.

The idea behind the Head Teacher's Award Series is much the same as the award-scheme practised in the classroom. This book has been devised for use by children who are coming up to their National Tests at the end of Key Stage Two. Not only does it reinforce all the information they need to know for their Tests through a series of fun and practical questions and activities, it gives children a chance to work a little harder and be rewarded with a Head Teacher's Award. Throughout the book, one or two questions on each page have a HTA symbol next to them, indicating that that particular question or activity may require a little more work or a more lateral approach in order to get the answer right. It is up to the parent to decide what the award should be (we are not advocating bribery here!), something to make the child feel they have reached a target. It may be that you decide with your child that they have to get a certain number of HTAs in the book before they can have their 'award', based on their ability.

Written by an author with great experience of Key Stage Two children, the aim of this book is that through a combination of revision, motivational aids and practical tests that the child can take in a familiar and comfortable environment, they will be as prepared as they can be for the National Tests that they will take at the end of Key Stage Two.

John Foster
Former Head Teacher of St Marks Junior School, Salisbury.

Introduction

What are SATs?

Children who are in Years 3 to 6 study Key Stage 2 of the National Curriculum. At the end of Year 6, in May, the children are tested on their knowledge and skills in three core subjects: Mathematics, English and Science. The tests are commonly known as SATs, which stands for Standard Assessment Tasks. The teachers use the SATs results, as well as continuous assessment that is conducted in the classroom, to assess how well the children are doing.

How this Book Works

By the time your child takes their SATs they should have covered everything in the National Curriculum that they are meant to know. This book is not intended to teach new subjects in English, but should be used as an aid to revision and improving exam technique. The book is divided into two main sections:

Revision Section

The essentials of the English curriculum are covered with clear explanations and examples. On the pages you will find key words or concepts highlighted to help your child remember them.

Parent's Guides

These feature regularly throughout the book and may:
- Explain why a topic is important
- Suggest what you can do to reinforce your child's learning of a topic
- Give examples of activities you can do together.

Questions

Quick questions feature throughout the book. By answering the questions your child will reinforce the concepts they have just covered in the text. Answering the questions correctly gives the children confidence and motivates them to continue working their way through the book.

Head Teacher's Award

Throughout the book Head Teacher's Award Questions (HTAs) feature. These are slightly harder than the other questions. Achieving a high standard in answering Head Teacher's Award Question earns your child the HTA.

Practice Papers

This is the section where your child can practise using the skills they have revised. There are four practice papers, including a Level 6 extension. These are explained in more detail on page 38. Answers and a marking scheme are included.

What You Can Do to Help

Encourage your child to complete the questions and activities **that are included in the revision section. Practice really consolidates learning and will be greatly beneficial to your child. Answering questions together will also help you identify any particular difficulties your child is having.**

Promote good learning habits **Encourage your child to plan their revision, allowing plenty of time for breaks. They will learn and retain more in two periods of 20 minutes with a five-minute break than an unbroken 45 minute period. Teach them to revisit a topic regularly, so that it becomes part of their long-term memory.**

Motivate your child to succeed **Reward your child for every HTA they get – discuss this with your child and agree a suitable reward.**

A healthy body keeps a mind active **Ensure that your child eats a well-balanced and healthy diet, gets plenty of exercise and a full night's sleep every night.**

Keep the tests in perspective **Remember that SATs are as much a test of the school's success as of your child's ability, so do not cause your child anxiety by over-stressing the importance of the exams. Nor are SATs an end in themselves; they are part of a whole process designed to ensure that your child has a solid foundation for later learning and success.**

Speaking and Listening

What Did you Say?

Think about listening to someone reading aloud or speaking aloud. What do they have to do so that you can hear, understand and enjoy what they are saying? This will remind you of the skills you need to do it well.

Speaking Up

You need to speak up so that the very furthest person in the room can hear you. Look around the room before you start so that you know how far your voice must carry. Don't be a shy flower, looking at your feet. Make sure they hear.

Question

You sometimes feel nervous when you are asked to speak. Do you think you are alone, or do others feel the same? Ask them.

Activity

Prepare a one-minute speech on why adults should listen to children's views. Present your speech to an audience and ask for feedback.

Getting the Right Speed

Speak at the right speed – not so fast that your audience miss the words and the meaning, or so slow that they all fall asleep.

Expression

Use plenty of **expression** so that everyone understands the sense of what you're saying, and the feelings behind the words.

Two Tips for Speaking Aloud

- If you have time, decide what you want to say beforehand. You can even make a note or two.
- Avoid rambling on and keep to the point. When you have said what you need to say, stop talking.

Parent's Guide

Good speaking and reading aloud need practice. Listen to your child from the furthest point in the room, then note their good points and tell them where they can improve. If they are difficult to understand, get them to deliver a passage in a loud whisper. It helps articulation and projection.

Tips for Discussion

Listen carefully to what others have to say. Try and get at what they are thinking, not what you think they are thinking.

Watch out for the signs that someone is finishing speaking. At the end they usually talk a little slower and lower their voices, or even look away.

Do not start speaking, or putting up your hand, until a natural pause. Then grab your chance.

Even if you have plenty of ideas, avoid hogging the discussion. Others have ideas too, and need the chance to express them. They may find this more difficult than you do.

Questions

1. How does the author show where pauses are needed when reading aloud?

2. When someone else is speaking, whose point of view is more important: yours or theirs?

Activity

Practise speaking and reading with a friend or friends. Give constructive criticism and praise each other.

Tips for Reading Aloud

• Practise reading ahead of the words you are saying at the time. If you do not know how the sentence ends then you may not get the sense or expression right. Read a familiar text initially to encourage confidence.

• Be ready to turn the next page before you come to it. Your listeners should not notice the page turning, because there is no break in your reading.

• Look at your listeners from time to time. That will remind you to speak up and encourage them to listen to you carefully. It makes you feel confident even if you are a bit scared.

• Remember to vary your voice. You can do this by speaking a little louder and softer, or faster and slower, according to the meaning. Never be dull. You can also vary your pauses.

Remember

How well you speak and read aloud is judged by your teacher, so your classroom work is important.

Reading and Comprehension

An Adventure Story

Read through this passage carefully, think of its meaning, think of how it makes you *feel*.

The Cave of Darkness

When at last they found the entrance to the secret cave, Meg and Phil stopped and looked inside. It was a black hole going deep into the mountain. Phil took a pace backwards.

'Do you think we really ought to go in?'

'Oh, don't be silly, Phil,' said Meg. 'We've finally got here, and I'm not going to stop now.'

They got out their torches, but somehow Phil seemed to have forgotten how to switch his on; Meg did it for him. Then, hand in hand, they took their first steps inside. As soon as they left the sunlight it felt cold and clammy. They both shivered. The beams of their torches were like searchlights, exploring the cave. The rock walls were craggy and wet, it looked as though no one had been there for a thousand years. In front of them the cave went around a corner, and so they crept forwards — the window of daylight behind them getting smaller and smaller and the darkness in front getting vaster and blacker. They turned the corner.

'What's that?' said Meg suddenly. Her torch was shining on what looked like the head of a huge man, not ten metres ahead. It glinted gold and green in the torchlight. She clutched on to Phil's arm. Then they heard a low, sad moaning. Was it just the wind or was it the head saying: 'Beware!'? Meg began to pull Phil back, they had to get out of there. But Phil stood his ground.

'I'm not going back,' he said. 'I'm not going to let the silly old wind stop me.'

But Meg had gone. Phil and the head were alone. His torch flickered and faded. It was pitch black except for a dull, greenish glow in front of him — and the moaning.

Parent's Guide

Children often rush at questions or give an answer to a question they think they know rather than what the questioner is asking. This will cost them marks. Think up some verbal questions like the ones on the opposite page, but ask your child to repeat the questions back to you before answering them.

Testing Questions

Here are some examples of the type of questions you may be asked in the Test, and how you might prepare your answers. The Test paper will indicate whether a short or long answer is needed.

You may be asked about the plot. For instance:

Had Meg and Phil been to the cave before? Find a clue that tells you this.

Look in the text. Your clue is 'At last they found the entrance'.

You may be asked to give examples that suggest feelings without actually describing them.

'Phil took a pace backwards'. What does this suggest about Phil's feelings?

You might answer: 'Phil felt suddenly frightened when he saw the cave entrance.'

You may be asked about characters.

Find a clue that suggests Meg was a kind person.

Look in the text for evidence. For instance, the clue to Meg's kindness is that she helped Phil with his torch.

You may be asked a general question.

Did you enjoy the story? Explain your reasons as fully as you can.

The answer here will be longer, perhaps ten lines. You might include details about the events, or the characters, or your opinion of mysterious adventure stories.

Questions

1. Phil was nervous at the beginning, but he stood his ground at the end. Was Phil brave or a coward? Give your reasons using evidence from the text to support your answers.

2. Why does the writer put a dash before the last few words?

Activity

Read the conversations (dialogue) out loud to yourself or a friend. Get the right expression through clues from the text. Include the head's windy 'Beware'.

Looking for Clues

When you read a story (that is, fiction) you should be aware of what is happening and your own feelings about it. What did the Cave of Darkness make you feel – boredom, excitement, fear, anticipation? Could you see the story in your mind's eye and really imagine that you were in the cave with Meg and Phil? Did you want to know what happened next, or were you happy that it was left to your imagination?

Now is the time for a little detective work, so get out your magnifying glass!

Think about Phil's character and his feelings. What sort of person is he? How does the writer reveal his character?

Look at the phrase that begins 'the window of daylight'. How does this give an idea of the length of the cave without telling us directly?

Look at the adverbs and the adjectives the writer has used. Why did Meg speak 'suddenly'? What picture does 'glinted gold and green' put into your mind?

The story has an air of mystery. Try and find two examples of how the writer suggests this.

Look for any other ways in which the writer makes the story effective.

Questions

1. Why do writers often leave you in mid air (called a 'cliffhanger') at the end of a chapter in a long book?

2. In the story, who speaks first? How do you know?

Activity

Cliffhangers are used in television programmes too, especially soap operas. Next time you watch a fiction programme, look for cliffhangers at the end of an episode or before the adverts.

Tip

If you can't remember the meanings of words such as 'adjective' or 'adverb', you can refer to the glossary on page 75.

Parent's Guide

Children's reactions to fiction are often quite definite, but tend to be general. Ask your child to give you their reasons for their reactions, and to point out concrete examples to back their views.

Giving Your Reasons

Remember that in your Test you will be asked to give actual examples to show how you have understood the story and how the writer has given you clues to the characters and their feelings.

Tips for Judging a Story

Look at a story before reading it. Does it look like a tempting read? Does the shape – like the length of the paragraphs or the conversation (dialogue) make you think it will be an easy read? Would you get a different impression if it were all in one paragraph?

Is the plot clear? Could you describe it in a line or two?

A story should leave you feeling that you know the main characters. Check how the writer tells you about them – through descriptions, the characters' actions and what they say.

Look at the conversations (dialogue). Do you always know who is speaking? Does the writer give clues to their tone of voice and their feelings?

How does the story end? Does it leave you wondering what will happen next, or bring it to a happy conclusion?

Questions

1. Why do you think Phil's problem with switching on the torch was mentioned?

2. Think of four words that could have been used instead of 'said'.

Activity

Look at the opening paragraphs of five fiction stories. Which ones have a good hook that make you want to read further?

Tip

A good writer tempts you into the story in the first line or two. This method is called the hook.

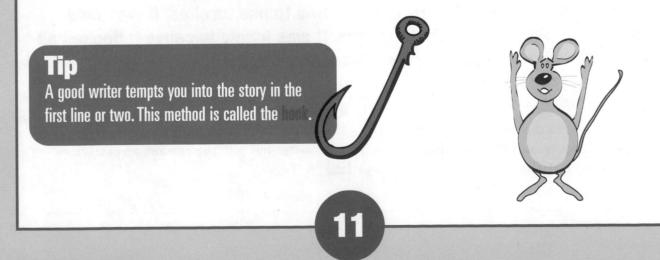

Good Ways to Answer Questions

Tips Before Starting

Read through the instructions at the beginning of the paper and follow them carefully. Ask your teacher if you do not understand.

Read each question carefully, asking yourself what the Tester wants to know and in what form the answer should be put. This is most important.

Some answers are a matter of opinion. Provided you give good reasons for your answer, it does not matter whether the Tester agrees with your opinion or not.

You do not have to answer the questions in order. If you meet a really difficult one, avoid getting stuck – answer easier questions, then come back to it later.

EXAMPLE:
Here is a question and a possible answer.

Q. What was it like inside the cave? Give reasons for your answer.

A. It was very dark because the children had to use torches. It was cold and clammy, and the walls were craggy. It was lonely because it 'looked as if there had been no one there for a thousand years'.

Question

Meg was brave enough to encourage Phil at the beginning, but what are the clues that she became frightened later?

Give your answer with evidence. You should use approximately 40–50 words.

Activity

Increase your vocabulary; every time you come across a new word, look for its meaning in a dictionary. Try to use the new word as often as you can.

Parent's Guide

Ask your child to choose a passage from a story they know well. Study the passage together as described opposite. and ask your child to note how the writer has got the passage across. (More about similes, metaphors and alliteration on page 18.)

Planning Your Answer

You will have plenty of time, so read the passage at least twice. The first time, read it like an ordinary story, then pause and think about what happened and how it made you feel. Then read it a second time, more slowly, noting how the writer has chosen to get the story across. You may like to underline words or phrases that seem important for this.

Read the questions carefully and make sure you know what the Tester is asking you for. Note whether a long or short answer is required.

Avoid giving general opinions. Try to be precise, and give good reasons for your views by quoting or summarising the passages or words that support your answers.

Think about the writer's use of language, and how it helps him tell the story.

Question
Summarise the story 'Cave of Darkness' You should use about 40–50 words.

Activity
Ask your friends about the stories they have read recently. Get them to tell you about the plot and the characters. Ask them to give you evidence to back up their opinions.

EXAMPLES:

- adjectives – is 'clammy' a more vivid and accurate adjective than 'wet'?
- adverbs – how does 'suddenly' add meaning to Meg's question?
- similes – 'torches were like searchlights'. Can you see them in your mind's eye?
- metaphors – the entrance is not really a 'window'. Would a simile have been less or more powerful?
- alliteration – 'It glinted gold and green'. Does this give the description strength?

Check your answers, including spelling and punctuation.

Tip
Answer the easier questions first and return to the hard ones later.

Remember
Look at the glossary on page 75 if you can't remember what these words mean.

Non-fiction

Non-fiction gives you information about things that are factual. There are many different kinds.

Biographies and autobiographies
These are accounts of people's lives. What does 'auto' mean?

Newspaper reports
These give an account of recent events. They are factual, but are they always true?

Reference sources, e.g. dictionaries, encyclopedias, atlases and telephone directories
Useful sources of potted information. You may need to look at more than one to find what you need. Is the information up to date?

Non-fiction books, textbooks and articles, including Internet pages
These are usually longer accounts of a particular subject. How might you check whether the writer knows his subject?

Questions
1. What is a glossary?

2. What is a thesaurus?

Activity
Look at the shelves in your school library. Make a list of the kinds of non-fiction you find.

Instructions
These tell you how to carry out a task.
Think of the last time you used instructions, perhaps to assemble a model or programme a video recorder. Were they clear and easy to follow?

Parent's Guide
Children often need help to research information. Devise some interesting questions like 'Who was Lord Nelson and what did he do?' or 'How do climbing plants cling to their supports?', and then do a joint exploration to find the answer. This might include a supervised Internet search.

Skimming and Scanning

Skimming and scanning are useful ways of quickly discovering what a book or article is about, and so getting at the information you need quickly.

Remember
Once you have found what you want, always check carefully that you have understood it properly.

Tips for Skimming

First, get a bird's eye view by checking through the material for clues like chapter headings and summaries, diagrams and illustrations.

Read quickly through the passages you need to get an overall picture.

When you have finished, pause and just repeat the main points in your head.

Tips for Scanning

Once you have found your way around the material by skimming, you will know where to look for the particular information you need.

Read through the material looking for the key words and ideas that you need.

Make notes where necessary, and use scrap-paper bookmarks if there are several pages.

Questions
1. What is the difference between the Contents and the Index of a book?

2. Where in a book do you normally find each of these?

Activity
With a friend, pick an article, about two pages long, which interests you. Each of you has five minutes to skim and scan. Then ask each other questions about it, alternately. Give yourselves two points for a correct answer, one for nearly correct. Notes may be used.

HEADTEACHER'S AWARD

Tip
Scribble one-word notes if you need to — never mark books or papers which are not your own (and even then only use a light pencil which you can rub out).

The Structure of Language

Sentences have different kinds of words in them, known as the parts of speech. In your test you will be expected to identify them.

- A noun is the name of a thing or a person.

The boy stood on the burning deck, and Frederick was his name.

- A pronoun stands in place of a noun so that you do not always have to repeat it.

He danced about with scream and shout. It burnt him just the same.

- A verb is a doing word. It tells you what the subject does or what is done to the subject. Verbs can have different tenses – normally past, present or future.

He looked on the inviting sea. 'I will not jump' he said.

- An adverb tells you about the way an action is performed. It qualifies a verb.

I'll search bravely for floating wood and sail safely to bed.

- An adjective describes, or qualifies, a noun

No floating wood nor rescue boat our frightened hero found. So no one knew his dreadful fate, but was he burnt or drowned?

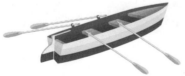

Question
In what tense is the word 'jump' in the example?

Activity
Look in an old magazine or newspaper and identify the different parts of speech you find there.

Reminder
Remember that an adverb qualifies a verb. What does an adjective qualify?

Parent's Guide
We all learnt parts of speech at school, but we haven't needed to identify them often since. So why not let your child teach you about them. Your child will learn too.

Hold Tight!

More parts of speech to come. You need to learn these ones too.

• **Prepositions** connect words to show position, direction and time. You'll find one of each, in that order, in the example.

Frederick stood beside the mast, he went towards the railings before he decided not to jump.

• **Conjunctions are 'joining words' like** but, and, although **and** because.

he looked over the railings and felt sick although the sea was calm.

• **The** definite **article is 'the' because it qualifies one noun. The** indefinite **article is 'a' or 'an' because it qualifies any one out of a number of nouns.**

Frederick searched through the ship in order to find a plank.

Question

noun

'Mary touched her quickly on her hand'. Find an adverb, two nouns, a verb, an adjective, a preposition and a pronoun in this sentence. Show which is which, just as the first noun is identified for you. (If you can get this all right, you're really good!)

Activity

Find out what a proper noun is and think of some examples.

Tip

If you really get stuck, a good dictionary will tell you what part of speech a word is. Sometimes the same word can be different parts of speech, depending on the work it is doing.

Think

If an adjective describes or qualifies a noun, are the definite and indefinite articles really adjectives?

Test Yourself

In the following passage, find one or more examples of all the parts of speech shown on these two pages.

Frederick really liked playing with matches and he never took notice of his mother's warnings. The family had a beautiful garden near the house, where he used to make fires. One day he carelessly left a little fire alight by some bushes. The bushes went up in a great flame because they were dry. His mother rushed out and angrily told Frederick that he would burn himself to death one day.

Reading Poetry

The study of poetry is one of the best ways to increase your English skills. It increases your vocabulary, gives you hidden meanings and conveys feelings – all in a short space. No wonder Testers like to include a poem.

Some of the Poet's Tools

As well as the tools of prose, poetry uses some special tools to get the right effect. They have to be kept very sharp indeed.

Rhyme

Many poems use rhyme, which often gives a good effect and makes them easier to remember. But rhyme is not always necessary. It depends on the poem.

Rhythm

The rhythm (or metre) of a poem is used to get across the feelings.

Simile

This is when a poet says that something is like something else, e.g. She's as beautiful as a butterfly.

Metaphor

This is when you say one thing is another. It is often more powerful than a simile. The line below contains a simile and a metaphor. Spot which is which.

His brow was like thunder, his eyes threw thunderbolts.

Alliteration

By using similar-sounding words, a poet can create an attractive effect.

Onomatopoeia

The poet uses words which sound like what he's saying, e.g. 'ding-dong' sounds like a bell.

Questions

This line contains alliteration and onomatopoeia:
The cheerful clatter of the cups.

1. Which letter is used for alliteration?

2. Which word is used for onomatopoeia?

Activity

Test the rhythm and patterns of different poems in your book and decide why the poet has chosen them.

Parent's Guide

Ask your child to read a poem out loud, then read it back to them. This way they get the sound of a poem. Help them to find examples of the poet's tools. Many children get confused about metaphors and need help to distinguish them from similes.

Types of Poetry

Poetry comes in all shapes and sizes. One poem may fill an entire book, another one may be two lines long. Some poems rhyme, others do not (blank verse). Poems can have complicated or simple patterns. Here are some accepted forms for poetry that you should know.

Haiku

This is a Japanese poem which has just three lines of five, seven and five syllables. It is usually about nature or the seasons, but it does not have to be.

Sonnet

This is a poem of 14 lines, each line usually containing ten syllables. Some poets use the last two lines to sum up the poem or point to a moral.

Ballad

This can be a longish poem that usually tells a story. Originally ballads were sung, and so the rhythm and the rhyme are suitable for this.

Look though your poetry book for these forms and others.

Haiku

With bejewelled feet
You tramp footsteps on my heart
Bruising the grasses.

Question

Compose a haiku. Count the syllables in the lines carefully. A haiku should not rhyme.

Activity

Complete the last line of this limerick, and read it out loud to check the rhythm.

There was an old codger from York
Who suddenly swallowed a fork
Once he chatted all day
Now he's nothing to say

Remember

A syllable is a sound within a word. The word syllable, for example, has three syllables: syll a ble.

Writing a story

Planning

Time spent on planning is well spent. Let's look at some of the stages.

What is the story about?
Your test paper will probably suggest a title or a subject, so jot down some random words starting from the title. You'll soon come up with an idea. Do you know what makes a good plot (storyline)? Think of Cinderella – that has a clear plot with a beginning, a middle and an end. It makes a complete story. Now plan and note the stages of your plot.

Who is the story about?
You need at least one character – it might be a person or an animal. Write down a very brief description of your main character or characters.

How long will the story be?
The test normally allows 15 minutes for planning and 45 minutes for writing. How much of this time will you need for checking and improving?

Remember
It's better to complete a short (but not too short) story than to leave a long one unfinished.

Question
Can you write down a character profile for an Ugly Sister?

Activity
Start the clock! Time how long it takes you to write and check a two-page story. Will you have time to write a rough draft first? Use this information to plan how long your story can be in the test.

Sample Character Profile
Cinderella: unloved stepdaughter, beautiful, black-haired, sad, teenager, kind, hopeful.

Parent's Guide
Pick a few possible titles and ask your child to think up a plot suitable for a two-page story. They may need help to get started, but during the Test they will have to do it on their own. If they can think up a handful of good storylines now they may be able to adapt one for the Test.

Features of a Good Story

Look out for the following points in planning and writing your story:

• **Interest** **your reader right from the start.**

Cinderella sat by the fire and wept. What a miserable evening she was going to have!

• **Help** **your reader to follow the plot. You will need to have planned a good structure for this.**

• **Allow your reader to see what is happening in their mind's eye.**

The embers of the fire were dark and cold. Cinderella shivered and hastily pulled her thin cloak about her shoulders.

• **You can also** suggest character **by actions and speech.**

Cinderella went up to her sister. 'Would you like me to pin up your hem?' she asked.

• **Go for a** good ending **which finishes the story off neatly.**

Question
Describe an angry man in two lines, using action and speech. No adverbs or adjectives allowed.

Activity
Describe the character of a member of your family. Use examples of speech and actions to help you. Can anyone recognise who you are talking about? If not, you'd better try again!

Tip
You can write a story in the first person (using 'I' and 'me') about yourself, but it should still indicate your character by description, thought and actions.

So Cinderella married her Prince, forgave her sisters and lived happily ever after.

Tip
The term D.A.D. is a useful way to remember what a good story needs to have: Dialogue, Action, Description.

Remember
Leave plenty of space between the lines/words so that you can make corrections clearly.

Improving and Checking Your Story

Writing a good story is not easy. Everyone can improve on their first attempt. Let's look at an extract from a story as it might have been first written.

When the found the entrance to the cave meg and Phil looked inside, it was big and dark. Phil shivered and said Do you think we ort to go in? Don't silly Phil, said Meg. We've finally got here and I'm not going to stop now..

They switched on their torshes then holding hands they went inside. In the dark it felt cold and miserable and they shivered.

Now go to page 8 and compare this extract with the writer's final draft. Try to spot the changes and work out why the writer made them.

Question

How many mistakes can you find in the extract above?

Activity

Make a list from the first draft above of misspellings, words left out and wrong capital letters. Everyone makes mistakes like this, which is why everyone has to check for them. Mistakes can cost you valuable marks.

Tip

It's wise to make an improved final draft instead of just correcting your first attempt, but check your timing by practice. See the 'Start the clock' Activity on page 20.

Parent's Guide

Look at some passages of dialogue in your child's storybooks. Discuss how the writer has set out dialogue and made it effective. Reading fiction is the best way for your child to become an imaginative writer.

Handling Speech

HEADTEACHER'S AWARD

Compare how the two drafts of the story handle speech.

Notice in the second draft (page 8) how each piece of dialogue has been given its own paragraph. This makes it easier to follow.

Each has been put in speech marks because it is writing what was actually said (direct speech). If it had read Phil asked whether they ought to go in, speech marks would not be used because this would tell us about what Phil said (indirect or reported speech), not what he said.

Question

Rewrite this conversation using correct speech marks and paragraphs.

It's raining again Tracey moaned. Her mother said Cheer up, Tracey! How can I, when it rains all the time?

Activity

'He shouted' might be an alternative to 'he said' in the right context. List five more verbs you could use as alternatives to 'said'.

Notice how the speaker is introduced. The first time Phil speaks, the writer has changed some words in the second draft just to indicate that Phil was speaking and to suggest what tone of voice he would have used. Compare the two drafts to see what was done.

If you are writing a longer conversation (dialogue) you should avoid using 'he said' or 'she said' all the time. Vary the ways you indicate who said what.

One way is to use adverbs or phrases that work as adverbs.

EXAMPLE:
. . . said Meg with irritation.

Or you can change the speaking word.

EXAMPLE:
. . . Meg snapped.

Be careful not to overdo this, though – just look out for natural opportunities.

When writing actual speech, match the expression to the character. Does 'Blow me, if it ain't Prince Philip on a 'orse!' said the Queen, sound right to you?

Story-telling Tools

There are many ways of making a rather dull piece of writing – like the first draft on page 22 – into something more vivid, more readable and with greater appeal to the imagination. Let's look at some of these ways.

- Look out for repeated important words, and try to find a variation. Notice that the word 'shiver' appears twice. How could you avoid the repetition? See the final draft (page 8) for one idea.

- Choose words that exactly convey your meaning. Phil's torch did not 'go out' (page 8), it 'flickered and faded'.

- Use the right adjectives – they lend colour and meaning to your writing. The cave was 'vast' not just 'big', the atmosphere was 'clammy'.

- Do the same for adverbs. Meg spoke 'suddenly'. And do not forget that you can use a phrase instead of a single word for adverbs and adjectives: 'Meg spoke with a choking voice' or 'Meg, who was kind to everyone'.

Question
'Nice' is a lazy word. Can you think of two alternative words that you could use?

Activity
Find an example of a simile, a metaphor and two examples of alliteration in the story on page 8.

Tip
Similes, metaphors and alliteration are common in poetry (learn more about these on page 18), but you should use them occasionally in ordinary writing, when you want to create a special effect.

Parent's Guide
Study a page from a story with your child. Discuss alternatives for some of the adverbs and adjectives. Discuss with your child whether they could be improved, or whether the writer has chosen the best or only ones.

Writing for Your Reader

What can you do to tempt people to read your work? Here are some suggestions.

- **Make the page look open and easy to read.** In the final draft, the writer has used short paragraphs and put in some conversation in order to do this.

- **Make your characters come across as live, interesting people (or animals, or aliens)** so that the reader can imagine what they are really like inside and want to find out what will happen to them.

- **A good beginning that 'hooks' the reader in is vital (see page 11). Unless you grab the reader at the start the rest will not matter.**

Ideas for Hooking the Reader

You could begin with a piece of conversation that leads the reader into the story.

'If only I could get rid of my shell,' sighed Topsy-Turvy, the tortoise, 'then I could run a little faster'.

You could begin with a statement which promises to lead on to something exciting.

The day before the world blew up, Tommy was sitting in the garden looking at the blue sky and watching a little cloud growing larger and angrier at every moment.

Question

Can you compose an opening to a story that would 'hook' a reader?

Activity

'Small', 'tiny', 'little', 'microscopic' are all words for the same idea, yet each has a slightly different meaning. Find three alternative words for 'big' that you might use in a story. Then try 'pretty' and 'angry'. What different shades of meaning do the alternatives have?

HEADTEACHER'S AWARD

Writing Non-fiction

In your test you may be asked to write something factual – that is, non-fiction. (Look at page 14 to see some different kinds of non-fiction). The basic rules for all composition are the same, but the style of writing may be different. Let's look at some examples.

Newspaper reports usually start with a short paragraph summarising the story – this is the 'hook'. The following paragraphs expand and give more detail. Sometimes a joke headline is used. Simple and vivid language is used to emphasise the news.

Monkey Business at the Zoo

At Middletown Zoo today a monkey escaped from his cage and stole 13 ice creams from horrified children. 'He didn't mean any harm but we're keeping him in, in future,' said zookeeper Brian Smith.

Ordinary non-fiction writing will vary. A serious subject needs serious language, but if, for instance, you were describing how you see yourself in 20 years time, then you would have more freedom in your style. Remember, though, that no writing should ever be dull. That's even more important in non-fiction because you cannot hold your reader's attention with the storyline.

In 20 years time I will have passed my 30th birthday, so by then I have got to succeed! Will I be captain of a space shuttle looking out on a small blue Earth? Will I be a millionaire computer whiz-kid designing fascinating games? Or will I be a down-and-out sleeping on the cold damp pavements of London?

Activity

Describe your favourite subject at school. Write 10-15 lines on scrap paper. Make sure your readers really understand why you like it, and begin to share your enthusiasm.

Warning!

In your Test you may be asked to write a letter. See how to do this on page 36.

Parent's Guide

Discuss the results of the activity above. Has your child really got their feelings across? Is the language bright and descriptive? Was the account clear? Suggest improvements if necessary. Encourage your child to broaden their reading to include non-fiction books.

Ten Rules for Composition

1. Question
Read the question and make sure you know what the Tester is asking you to do.

2. Preparation
Good preparation is vital for good composition. You dare not skip it.

3. Content
Note down what you are going to say – the main plot if it is a story, the key points if it is non-fiction. Every composition has a beginning, a middle and an end.

4. Characters
If you are writing fiction, decide on your characters (probably not more than three for a story) and what they are like.

Question
Write a 'hook' (two or three lines) for an article called 'Why I love tests'. That's a challenge!

5. Hook
Decide how you are going to 'hook' your reader.

Activity
Learn the main points of the rules before you go to sleep tonight. Each one has a key word to help you. Repeat them when you wake up.

6. Length
Now that you know how long it takes, decide on approximate length and whether to use a first, rough draft.

7. Layout
Remember to lay out your work neatly and keep your paragraphs short but varied.

8. Tools
Use the tools of good writing to give interest and to create pictures in your reader's mind.

Remember
Which two of the rules of composition are you most inclined to forget? How are you going to remember them in the Test?

9. Improve
Now check what you have written, first for silly mistakes and then for ways to improve your writing. No one has ever written a draft that cannot be improved.

10. Double check
Finally, check again for silly mistakes, for example the incorrect use of a capital letter.

Punctuation

You need punctuation to make your meaning clear and your work easy to read. Good punctuation means more marks.

Full Stops

Full stops are easy. They end every sentence. The next sentence begins with a capital letter.

Commas

Commas are tricky. You have to use them all the time – to help your meaning and to break up long sentences. A good tip for commas is to read a sentence out loud to yourself. Where you need a pause, you probably need a comma. But check if a new sentence would be better.

Question

Can you punctuate the following sentence?

Mum took the food over to the baby and fed it she also took a beaker a bib and a spoon

Activity

Vital Revision

Sorry! You'll just have to revise what you learnt in class and from your textbook. Study how to use commas in lists. Look at where you should, and should not, use commas to break up sentences, or make them clear.

Question Marks

These are easy. They come at the end of questions instead of a full stop. Remember not to use them when the question is only reported and not put directly. 'Phil wondered whether they should go into the cave' should not have a question mark.

Exclamation Marks

These replace full stops when you want to express strong feelings. For example: 'Stop!' or 'What a wonderful day!' Be mean with exclamation marks. Only use them when they are really necessary.

Parent's Guide

Some children use virtually no punctuation, others scatter it at random. Show them how it is a mixture of rules and common sense, perhaps using a storybook to illustrate. Check that they have revised the use of commas (see above).

Speech Marks

The first rule is easy. When you are writing the actual words that someone is saying, use speech marks at either end.

The second rule is trickier. When the speech has its own punctuation at the end, put the speech marks outside it. Thus: 'I'll have your guts for garters!' shouted Jimmy.

But no speech marks are needed for: Jimmy said he thought I was an idiot. Why?

Quotation Marks

These are similar to speech marks, and sometimes people use "quotation marks" for both. You sometimes need quotation marks in non-fiction in order to show you are quoting from something else, not necessarily speech.

Remember the warning on the last page: "Good punctuation means more marks".

Notice how the punctuation here is for the whole sentence, so it goes outside the quotation marks.

Questions

1. Put the commas in the correct places in this list:
Ice cream cakes trifles and bread and butter.

2. Which sentence is correct?
Astronauts who are stupid make mistakes.
Astronauts, who are stupid, make mistakes.

Activity

Look at conversations (dialogues) in a storybook. Note how the writer has used punctuation.

Brackets

Brackets are useful, particularly in non-fiction, when you want to insert extra information into a sentence.

Evergreens (trees which keep their leaves in winter) should be a part of every garden.

Apostrophes

Apostrophes, which look like single speech marks, have two main uses.

Turning two words into one:

do not	don't
I will	I'll
Is not	isn't
Have not	haven't
They are	they're

In such cases, and there are many others, the apostrophe replaces one or more letters. Do not use these shortened forms in formal writing – and that means in your Test answers. You can, however, use them in conversations (dialogue) in your stories, because this is how we speak. You can also use them in poetry, where they are sometimes needed to get the rhythm (metre) right.

To show ownership:
For most words an 's is added.

John's mobile
The cat's pyjamas
The horse's head

Remember
Plural nouns like mice, women and children use an 's because they are single words: mice's nests; children's games.

When a single word already ends in an s you can add an apostrophe and an extra s, or you can put an apostrophe after the last s in the word.
Mrs Jones' dog or Mrs Jones's dog

For plural ownership words use s'.
The cats' pyjamas
The horses' heads

Parent's Guide
Apostrophes, like almost every other rule in English, have their exceptions, and your child will have learnt some of these at school. A common mistake is to use 's in ordinary plurals, such as dog's like walks. There are a surprising number of adults who make mistakes with apostrophes — help your child to master this subject now.

Sentences, Paragraphs and Speech Layout

When you are writing, make the page look open and easy to read with your sentences, paragraphs and speech.

Sentences

You should vary the length of sentences as this makes your writing easier to read. Avoid very long sentences, even if you are an expert in punctuation. Sometimes short sentences are used to get a special effect:

He drew the gun. He aimed. He pulled the trigger. Nothing happened.

Paragraphs

A paragraph contains sentences which naturally go together or follow on from each other. Like sentences, you should vary their length – though a paragraph can contain just one sentence. Paragraphs make your meaning clearer and your work easier to read.

Tip

A paragraph should always start on a new line. Always leave a space (about 1.5 cm) when starting the first line of a paragraph.

Question

Can you make a list – as long as you can – of words with a letter or letters missing, like 'don't'? Get your apostrophes in the right place.

Activity

Write a sentence 20 to 30 words long. Be sure the punctuation makes it easy to read. Now see if you can split it into two sentences. You may have to change a word or two to do this. Is it easier to read now?

Laying Out Speech

Speech (dialogue) should always have a new paragraph for each speaker. Check for rules and tips on pages 11, 24 and 29. Sometimes you can get away with a very short speech within a paragraph.

Spelling

You can lose marks in the Test for poor spelling. Learn the following rules:

- **Remember** i before e except after c – but only if it rhymes with tree. **So deceit (because the ei part rhymes with tree) but** science **(because it does not).** Seize, weird **and** weir **are exceptions you need to learn.**

- **It often help to split long words in your mind into their parts.** Backbone **splits into which two parts? Would this help if you were writing** unnecessary**? Watch out for words like** careful**. When the second part ends with -ull (care-full) you need to drop the second** l**.**

- **Only one** c **is necessary, but two are required for su**cc**ess.**

Tip
Many spelling mistakes are made simply through not thinking. Check for silly mistakes.

Question
A friend has asked you to check their spelling. Make the corrections. Cross out incorrect words with a neat line, and write the correct spelling above, just as you will in your Test. Be neat!

Im riting this storey carfully. Its about a wierd freind called Kieth, who is decietful and not a sucess at scool.

Activity
If you have been sensible you will have kept a list of words you find difficult. Revise it now! If you have no list, get cracking and make one, than add to it every time you make a spelling mistake.

Parent's Guide
Ask your child to show you their spelling or vocabulary book, and encourage them to add to it continually. Use the book as the basis for quizzes. If your child has no spelling or vocabulary book, make sure they start one. (See the activity on page 12.) With your child, go through previous written work and list their misspelt words.

Plurals

Although most single words are made plural by simply adding an s (dog becomes dogs), there are some tricky ones. Here are some helpful guides.

- Words which end in y: when the letter before the y is a vowel, the word is made plural in the usual way. So boy becomes boys. If the letter before is a consonant, you use -ies. So company becomes companies. This does not apply to proper names. There are three Henrys in my class, not three Henries.

- Some single words end in a hissing sound, for example box, witch, grass. To make these plural add -es: boxes, witches, grasses. A good tip is to say the word to yourself and see if it sounds right with the e put in.

Most words which end in o are made plural by simply adding an s. But others need -es. Here are some common examples:

pianos	potatoes
zeros	heroes
photos	volcanoes
memos	tomatoes

Most words ending in f or fe should usually be changed to -ves to make them plural. Here are some common words which cause difficulties:

Singular	Plural
elf	elves
half	halves
handkerchief	handkerchiefs
knife	knives
leaf	leaves
life	lives
proof	proofs
wife	wives

Activity

Study the guides on this page and the word lists. Now see if you can answer the Head Teacher's Award problem below without referring back. Afterwards, check against the guides.

Question

Turn each highlighted word below into the plural. Cross out the original word neatly and write the plural word above. Take care!

I watched the cargo of loaf of bread being unloaded from the ship. I remembered story I had heard about volcano erupting so close to the sea that the man on board had to wipe their eye with their handkerchief. The mouse on deck were so excited that they danced calypso with Captain O'Reilly and the First Mate, together with their wife. The O'Reilly were very good dancers.

Handwriting

Some lucky people have naturally neat handwriting, but most of us have to practise hard in order to be neat. It is important not only because you will have a Handwriting Test, but also because you are likely to lose marks in any written work which the Tester cannot read easily. Here are some tips.

- Get into the habit of always writing neatly – even for your rough work. You will soon find with practice that good handwriting can be done just as quickly as poor handwriting.

Activity

In your best handwriting, copy a passage of about 10 lines from a book on to lined paper, remembering the tips above. Check against your other written work and see where you have improved.

- Always write on the line - do not wave up and down like the sea.

  do not write like This – but like this

- Keep good spaces between the words, and make your spacing roughly equal.

  notlike this but like this

- Form your letters clearly. Some people have the habit of writing particular letters badly. If you cannot spot these for yourself, your teacher or your parents will help you.

- Capital letters should be bigger than your ordinary letters, and a tiny bit bigger than tall letters like d or b.

  Cde

- You can write with straight up-and-down letters or on a slant, but you must keep all your letters in the same direction.

  do not write Like This – but like this

- Correct your mistakes with neat crossing through, and write the correct word above.

  do not correct like th̶i̶s̶ – but like ~~this~~ this

Parent's Guide

Good handwriting is not acquired overnight, so the earlier the start and the more the practice, the better. The emphasis should be on encouragement for even minor improvements rather than nit-picking, so that your child begins to take pride in good handwriting rather than seeing it as a chore.

34

If you are left-handed then following the rules of handwriting can be more difficult. You need to find your own technique to keep your writing neat. Look on the bright side – left-handers are supposed to be very creative, so what you lose in neatness you should make up for in imagination!

Abigail is someone who finds neat writing difficult. The 'before' example is taken from her ordinary writing, and the 'after' example is a copy she made when she had been practising better handwriting. Which would you rather read?

Abigail 'before'

> The story is based on a little girl, 'Alice' who goes ~~throf~~ through a looking glass and finds herself

Abigail 'after'

> The story is based on a little girl, 'Alice' who goes through a looking glass and finds herself in

Question

Copy the following passage, paying special attention to the handwriting points you have revised. If you make a mistake, remember how to cross out neatly. Do not forget what you learned about paragraphs on page 31. 'Czar' is the Russian name for 'emperor'.

Every night the Firebird would visit the Czar's garden and steal a golden apple from his favourite tree. By the morning the bird would be gone.

The Czar was furious. He sent for his three sons and ordered them to ride to all the corners of Russia, to find the Firebird, and to bring it back unharmed.

....

....

....

....

....

Activity

Even Abigail 'after' is not perfect, but she is really improving. Pretend you are her teacher and write down the ways in which you think she has improved, and what she might do to improve further. (Notice that she has forgotten the comma which should come after 'Alice'.)

Formal and Informal Letters

Formal Letters

- Formal letters have some special rules which you will have been taught in class or studied in your textbooks. Here are some reminders, which you should compare with the example opposite.

- Your best handwriting is fine, or you can use a word processor.

- Write your own address at the top right-hand side.

- Write the name (or title) and address of the person to whom you are writing below this, but on the left-hand side. Opposite this, put the date.

- Address the person concerned as, for example, 'Dear Mr Woggins' or, if you do not know the name, 'Dear Sir or Madam'. Remember that abbreviations like 'Mr' or 'Dr' do not need a full stop because they end with the same letter as the full word.

- Under this, write in the subject of your letter, and underline it.

- Set out your letter clearly and use formal but natural language. Remember your paragraphs.

- End your letter correctly. Use 'Yours sincerely,' if you have used someone's name at the start of the letter or 'Yours faithfully,' if you have started 'Dear Sir or Madam'.

Question

Translate the following into formal language.

Your computers are cool but I don't think they're lightning quick.

Activity

Practise writing letters on a word processor, then print them out to check them. Experiment with your software's tools to change the appearance of the letters.

Parent's Guide

Look at some formal letters (not private ones) which you have received and discuss with your child whether they have been written correctly.

Sample Formal Letter

27 Gringe Road
London
SW19 4LP

23 November 2002

Henry Woggins
Sales Manager
Beemer Toys
East Beemer
RG21 2DZ

Dear Mr Woggins,

Re. My order no. 67A4320 - The Witches of Wimbledon Game

I am returning this game to you because it is the version for a Doors ME computer, and it will not work properly on my machine.

As I wrote in my letter of 10 November, my computer uses Doors 95.

Would you please send me the correct version or, if that is not available, refund my payment. The cost was £39.99 plus my postage costs of £3.50.

Yours sincerely,

M. Pecksniff

Mabel Pecksniff (Miss)

Informal Letters

These are much easier. Although they should contain your own address, and should be written and set out neatly, you should use less formal and more friendly language. You should not put in your friend's address, and you do not need to write your name out again carefully unless no one can read your signature. (Or, better still, change your signature!)

Question

Using a separate sheet of paper, write out Mr Woggins' reply to Miss Pecksniff, apologising for the error, and saying you will send her, within a few days, a version of the game which will work on Doors 95. You do not need to type the letter, but use your best handwriting. Make up any details you need.

Activity

Write an informal letter to your friend Bill, thanking him for inviting you to his birthday party last week, and saying how much you enjoyed yourself. Sign with your first name or nickname. Make up any details you need.

Introduction to Practice Test Papers

The National Tests

Children at the end of Key Stage Two (Year Six) take tests in English, maths and science. Each subject in the National Curriculum is divided into core subjects.

In English, for example, these are:

* Speaking and Listening
* Reading
* Writing
* Handwriting and Presentation

Targets are set for achievement within these core subjects.

In English, for example, 'Writing' includes:

* Composition, planning and drafting
* Punctuation and spelling
* Handwriting and presentation
* Standard English and Language Structure

A combination of written tests (SATs or NCTs) and continuous classroom assessment enables the teachers to record the targets individual children have met.

What do SATs involve?

The children are given written papers to complete. In English they have three or four papers:

The Reading Test is 60 minutes long. The first 15 minutes are spent studying the reading booklet. 45 minutes are spent writing answers in a separate answer booklet. This test assesses levels 3–5.

The Writing Test is 60 minutes long. The first 15 minutes are spent choosing one out of four possible pieces to work on, then planning them. This test assesses levels 3–5.

The Spelling and Handwriting Test involves a short dictation (10 minutes) and a short passage for the children to copy out.

The Extension Paper is given to children who are expected to achieve level 5 very easily. It assesses them to Level 6 and lasts for 60 minutes.

How are National Tests marked?

Children sit the exams in May and the test papers are sent away for marking. Results come back in July.

- Most children will achieve results between Level 3 and Level 5.
- Level 3 indicates that extra work is required to reach the target for this age group.
- Level 4 indicates that targets set for this age group have been attained.
- Level 5 or above indicates that the targets for their age group have been exceeded.
- Generally, children are expected to move up one level every two years.

What are SATS Results used for?

SATs results may indicate several things:
- Whether a child is progressing through the levels appropriately.
- Whether a school is doing well.
- Areas of weakness that a child might need extra help with.
- SATs results may also be used, with other assessments, to help Year 7 teachers decide how to allocate children to suitable ability groups or classes.

How Should I Use the Practice Papers?

In this section of the book you will find examples of all four types of test. Your child should not attempt to take any of the tests until they have, at least, skimmed through the revision section and answered the questions they encountered on the way. In some instances, the tests here are slightly shorter than the ones they will have in the real Test.

It can be de-motivating to do badly in a test. Ensure your child has a good understanding of the concepts and techniques used in each Practice Paper before they attempt it.

Encourage your child to complete a Practice Test paper in real exam conditions. This means no help, no breaks and only the equipment allowed in the instructions to the Test.

Answers are at the back of the book. It is essential that you help your child to correct any mistakes they make. Heap plenty of praise on them for the work they complete correctly, and reward them for good corrections that are done promptly.

If your child continues to struggle with a subject, you should discuss this with their teacher, who may be able to suggest an alternative way of helping your child.

Test 1: Writing Test (Levels 3–5)

Instructions

The reading texts you will need appear at the beginning of this section. They are:

The Legend of Theseus and the Minotaur
The poem: Sir Galahad
Chinese Myths and Legends

Before you begin the written part of the Test, you should take ten minutes to read and study these carefully, including the notes which are given. You can refer back to these texts while you are answering the questions.

> In the real Test the readings are given in a separate leaflet. They will be similar but longer than those in your Practice Test, and you will have 15 minutes in which to read them.

In the written part you will be asked different kinds of questions, and you will see the maximum number of marks that can be given. Questions that require a written answer will show you whether your answer should be long or short by the number of lines allowed; 45 minutes are allowed for the written part.

There will also be:
- Questions which require you only to tick or ring the best answer from a choice of four.
- Questions which ask you to show connected words or phrases by linking them with a drawn line.
- Questions which ask you to write simple phrases or sentences.
- Questions which ask your opinion, supported by good reasons from the text. These require the longest answers.

Notice the number of marks that can be given for each question. One mark means that the answer will be simple – usually a single word or short phrase; two marks mean either that two or more pieces of information are required, or that the question needs more thought; three marks mean that the question requires a longer answer and even more thought.

You may use a pen or a sharp pencil. Make your corrections neatly – rubbing out is allowed.

The Legend of Theseus and the Minotaur

Theseus was one of the bravest of the Greeks, yet his story ended sadly. He was the son of King Aegeus of Athens, and King Aegeus had a real problem. Every ninth year the Athenians had to send seven young men and seven young women to King Minos of Crete, who would kill them all in a particularly horrible way.

Prince Theseus volunteered to deal with the problem and he travelled to Crete in a ship with black sails. He told his father that if he succeeded he would change the sails to white so that his father would see them and know that he had returned alive and in triumph.

When he arrived he was arrested and told that he would be fed to the Minotaur – a huge monster that had the head of a bull and the body of a man. The Minotaur lived in a deep lair which was so filled with twistings, turnings and different passages that once you had entered you could never find your way out. It was a maze called the Labyrinth – a word we still use today.

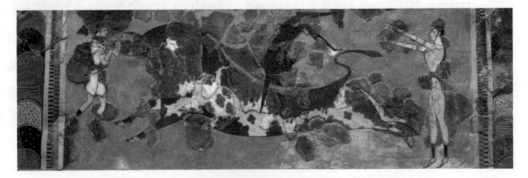

Although Theseus was a hero he felt very nervous, but luckily Ariadne, the beautiful daughter of King Minos, found him a sword and gave him a ball of thread. While she held one end, Theseus would unwind the ball and in this way he would be able to find his way back to the entrance. Ariadne's smile made him feel even more courageous and more determined to succeed.

Inside the Labyrinth, Theseus moved forward carefully. In a moment he was lost, but luckily he was still unwinding the thread. As he searched further and further he could only hope that the thread would be long enough. What if he ran out before he found the Minotaur – or the Minotaur found him? In the distance he heard a bellow echoing around the passages. Theseus ran towards the noise but found himself going round and round until, suddenly, he came face to face with the Minotaur.

It was huge – with fierce red eyes, a black hairy head and great horns with points as sharp as spears. It let out a huge bellow and charged, aiming its horns straight at Theseus' stomach. But Theseus was quick; he seized the horns and somersaulted right over the beast's back. For a moment the Minotaur paused. Where had his prey gone? Theseus seized his chance and thrust his sword up to the hilt in the Minotaur's heart. The beast was dead; he would kill no more Greeks. Theseus returned safely to Ariadne, winding up the thread as he went.

As Theseus sailed back to Greece his mind was full of his adventure and he was thinking about Princess Ariadne. He was so distracted that he forgot to change his sails from black to white. When King Aegeus looked out from a cliff towards the horizon, he saw his son's ship returning – but it had black sails. In his despair he threw himself off the cliff, and the sea in which he was drowned is called the Aegean Sea to this day. You can find it in your atlas.

Note: Crete is a large island about 200 km south of Greece. In the ruins of the ancient palace at Knossos you can still see the sign of the bull horns, and wall pictures of athletes vaulting the bull — just as Theseus did. Some people think that the palace, which had so many rooms you could get lost in it easily, was the origin of the Labyrinth.

Sir Galahad

Sir Galahad was one of King Arthur's most virtuous knights. In this poem we read about him taking part in a tournament where knights fought against each other in front of a large excited audience. The knights were like pop stars and the young women had their favourites with whom they thought they had fallen in love. This is just the first verse of the poem.

My good blade carves the casques of men,
My tough lance thrusteth sure,
My strength is as the strength of ten,
Because my heart is pure.
The shattering trumpet shrilleth high,
The hard brands shiver on the steel,
The splinter'd spear-shafts crack and fly,
The horse and rider reel:
They reel, they roll in clanging lists,
And when the tide of combat stands,
Perfume and flowers fall in showers,
That lightly rain from ladies' hands.

Lord Tennyson (1809–92)

casques	**knights' helmets covering the whole head**
brands	**in this poem 'brands' are sword blades that flashed like fire**
lists	**the battles in the tournament**

44

Chinese Myths and Legends

The Chinese have a story about P'an Ku, who was the first man. He was a god-like giant who worked for eighteen thousand years to bring order to the Universe. When he died, his head turned into a mountain, his breath became the cloud and wind, and his voice became the thunder. The insects and other creatures that fed off his body turned into the race of men and women.

P'an Ku was followed by three ages: the Heaven Kings, the Earth Kings and the Man Kings. The Man Kings had the faces of men and the bodies of dragons. To this day the Chinese use dragons as an important element in their ceremonials. It was during this time that men learnt the art of eating and drinking; and the first calendar was made.

Following this, new arts began to develop. Sui Jin, or the 'firemaker', learnt how to use fire by watching the sparks fly as the birds pecked the trees. Yu Ch'ao lived in nests and built the first house. Many other arts, such as dancing and cooking, were developed.

Then came the Five Rulers. These are claimed to be historical, but when you hear that the first ruler Fu Hsi (he is supposed to have lived around 3000 BC) still had the body of a dragon, and had six dragons as counsellors, you can see how myth and history get mixed up. The Five Rulers each had different characters, and during their reigns agriculture, silk weaving, musical instruments, ploughing and many others arts were discovered.

Fung Hsi invented the art of writing, using pictures instead of letters. The Chinese still write using pictures today. Some legends tell us that Yen Ti, one of the rulers, had a glass front to his body so that he could see how his insides worked. Not surprisingly, he made many discoveries in medicine.

Here are some examples of Chinese writing. Can you see how pictures are used to form the words?

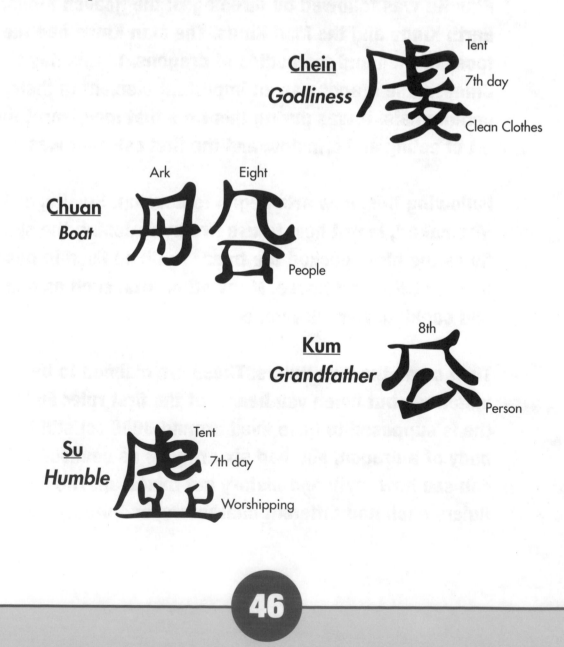

Chein
Godliness
Tent
7th day
Clean Clothes

Chuan
Boat
Ark
Eight
People

Kum
Grandfather
8th
Person

Su
Humble
Tent
7th day
Worshipping

Reading Test

These questions are about The Legend of Theseus and the Minotaur.

Put a tick in the box next to the best answer.

1. The Minotaur was:

1 MARK

- a bull ☐
- a giant ☐
- part bull, part man ☐
- a coal miner ☐

2. The Minotaur's voice was like:

1 MARK

- a bellow ☐
- a great shout ☐
- a low moan ☐
- a moo ☐

3. Theseus' ship had:

1 MARK

- red sails ☐
- white sails ☐
- no sails ☐
- black sails ☐

4. Theseus was armed with:

a ball of thread ☐

a sword ☐

spearpoints ☐

a bull-catcher ☐

Write your answer on the line or lines below each question.

1 MARK

5. The Minotaur had fierce red eyes. Why does the author put in this detail?

....

....

....

2 MARKS

6. Find a clue in the second paragraph that Theseus cared about his father's feelings.

....

....

2 MARKS

7. The Minotaur lived in the Labyrinth which was like a maze. Why did he have this for his lair?

....

....

8. How did Theseus feel about Ariadne? Give two clues from the given text to support your answer and write it below.

3 MARKS

....

....

....

....

9. Match the list of characters with the feelings they have. Draw a line from the character to the feeling.

2 MARKS

King Aegeus   Determined to be brave

Minotaur   Worried

Theseus   Fierce and furious

10. Why was it a mistake for Theseus to forget about changing his sails when he returned?

2 MARKS

....

....

11. Some words which we use nowadays come from the old myths. Find such a word in the story and write it in the box below.

1 MARK

2 MARKS

12. Why did Ariadne give Theseus the ball of thread?

....

....

3 MARKS

13. Legends often have a foundation in fact. Look in the last paragraph and the note that follows it for three clues to Theseus and the Minotaur that you can see today.

....

....

3 MARKS

14. Give your opinions on The Legend of Theseus and the Minotaur.

Remember, you are marked on the good reasons you give for your opinions, not on what your opinions are.

Think about:
Did you enjoy the story or not?
Did you like the characters?
Did the story make you want to read to the end?
Was the story easy to understand?

....

....

....

....

....

These questions are about the poem **Sir Galahad.**

1 MARK

1. What weapons does Sir Galahad use in the tournament?

....

1 MARK

2. Why do perfume and flowers rain from ladies' hands?

....

1 MARK

3. Sir Galahad has the strength of ten. From where does this strength come?

....

1 MARK

4. When writers say that something is like or similar to something else it is called a simile. Find an example of a simile in the poem.

....

2 MARKS

5. When writers use a word or a phrase in a way which is different from its ordinary meaning in order to make their ideas more vivid, it is called a metaphor. Flowers do not really fall as **rain**, so rain is a metaphor. Find two other metaphors in the poem.

....

....

2 MARKS

6. When writers choose a word which sounds like what they are saying, it is called onomatopoeia (pronounced on-o-mat-o-pee-a). The word shrilleth is used to sound like the high call of a trumpet. Find two other onomatopoeic words in the poem.

....

....

2 MARKS

7. When writers choose to use words with a similar sound close together, it is called alliteration, e.g. his mother bathed the bonny babe. Find two examples of alliteration in the poem.

....

....

3 MARKS

8. Describe your feelings when you read the poem and how the poem makes you feel this way. Feelings are always personal, so your reasons for your feelings are important.

Think about:
The character of Sir Galahad.
The sense of battle taking place.
How the poet uses words or phrases to give you feelings.
The rhythm, or metre, of the poem.
Does the rhyming contribute to the poem? How?

....

....

....

....

These questions are about the article on Chinese Myths and Legends.

1 MARK

1. When P'an Ku died he became the origin of three things. Match the list of P'an Ku's parts with what they became. Draw lines to show which goes with which.

his head   cloud and wind

his breath   thunder

his voice   mountain

1 MARK

2. In the myth, where did the race of men and women come from?

....

1 MARK

3. From where does the article suggest Yen Ti learned his medical knowledge? Ring the answer you think is correct.

books   his ancestors   watching birds peck   his see-through body

2 MARKS

4. Give two examples from the myth of customs or skills which the Chinese in particular still use today.

....

....

2 MARKS

5. How did Yu Ch'ao invent houses?

....

....

1 MARK

6. Although the first ruler may have actually existed, what are the clues that history and mythology were mixed?

....

....

2 MARKS

7. List five arts or skills which, according to the myth, the Chinese discovered.

....

....

....

....

....

1 MARK

8. Looking at the Chinese writing character; what kind of writing instrument do you think was used? Ring the answer you think is correct.

pen and ink   brush and ink   ballpoint   pencil

3 MARKS

9. Given that the ancient Chinese had very little scientific knowledge, do you think that their myths and legends about the beginning of the world and the discoveries of man were quite sensible or just foolish? Give your reasons, with examples from the article.

Think about:
Whether humans need explanations for their origins.
How well the stories explained the world they knew.

....

....

....

....

....

....

Test 2: Spelling and Handwriting

Spelling Test

Note to parent: the full transcript of this passage is on page 78.

Instructions

This test will last about 10 minutes. An adult will read a passage to you (see note above). Follow the passage below as they read it. When the adult reads the passage a second time, write the correct word in each gap. If you are not sure how to spell the word, try to write what you can.

Michael loves playing with his younger ...., Sam and Luke, but he always gets into................. Last .... Michael's mother took the three boys on a .... day out to a safari park. As ...., the day started well but it wasn't long before the younger boys began to be ....

Sam and Luke .... their ice-cream wrappers over the fence, into the giraffe's .... Michael knew it was a bad thing to do, so when his mother's back was turned he .... over the fence to .... the wrappers. The keeper saw Michael standing next to the giraffe. He was.................

No one was .... in Michael's .... and the other boys just stood behind a tree, giggling. The keeper suggested Michael be punished for his .... and his mother agreed. Poor Michael spent the rest of the day .... piles of muck out of an empty .... cage. Sam and Luke, ..., got to see all the animals.

The following week Luke and Sam's mother offered to take Michael to the .... Needless to say, Michael refused. He .... it would be much safer to stay at home and watch .... on his own.

Handwriting Test

Instructions

Here is a short paragraph that finishes the passage. Write it out very neatly in your own handwriting. You will be given a mark for your handwriting. Remember to make your writing as neat as possible, joining your letters if you can.

Michael's experience at the safari park was not all bad. Although the task he was given was unpleasant, it gave him plenty of time to think and watch the animals in the nearby cages. It helped Michael realise that he wanted to work with animals when he left school.

Test 3: Writing

Instructions and Planning Sheets

You must choose one piece of writing from the four in this test.

1. A Tale of Bravery
2. The Quest
3. Leisure Centre
4. Summer Fun

An adult should read this section with you.

The section also contains some planning pages to help you organise your ideas.

You will have 15 minutes in which to think about what to write and make a note of your ideas.

There are three pages (pages 66 to 68) for you to write your story on.

You will have 45 minutes to do your writing.

A Tale of Bravery

Write a traditional tale about an imaginary hero or heroine.

You will need to decide:
- **Who the main character is.**
- **What brave actions he or she carries out.**
- **How the story ends.**

PLANNING SHEET

This is for very brief notes to help you plan your ideas.
Your notes will not be marked.

Remember to think about:
- **The characters in your tale.**
- **How to start your tale.**
- **What the acts of bravery are.**
- **How to end your tale.**
- **The way traditional tales are written.**

A Quest

Here is part of a story:

> The Queen was worried: her husband, the King, had not returned from his travels to the Land of Lost Children. She asked her daughter, Princess Pia to follow his trail. Princess Pia knew it was her duty to find her father and she set off through the Forbidden Forest.

Pia had to find her father and rescue him from the trouble he was in.

Write the story of Pia's journey through the Forbidden Forest and how she found and rescued her father.

You will need to decide:
- **Where the King was and what kind of trouble he was in.**
- **How Pia rescued him.**

PLANNING SHEET

This is for very brief notes to help you plan your ideas. Your notes will not be marked.

Details about where the King is	
Other characters involved	

Remember to think about:
- **How to start the story.**
- **The most important events in your story.**
- **How to end your story.**

Note: do not spend time copying out the beginning of the story.

Leisure Centre

You have discovered that your local leisure centre has decided to increase its charges. This means that many of your friends will no longer be able to attend the swimming lessons there; they are just too expensive.

You want to write a letter to the manager of the leisure centre.

You have to persuade the manager to reduce the charges.

You will need to decide:
- **Why the swimming lessons are important.**
- **Why the costs should be reduced.**
- **What the manager could do instead to save money.**

PLANNING SHEET

This is for very brief notes to help you plan your ideas. Your notes will not be marked.

First, make some notes:

Why swimming lessons matter:

1..

2..

3..

Why the prices should be reduced:

1..

Other ways to save or raise money:

1..

2..

Remember to think about:
- **How to begin your letter.**
- **How to organise your points.**
- **What details to include.**
- **How to persuade the manager.**
- **How to end your letter.**

Summer Fun

During the Easter holidays you took part in an activity week for children. You have been asked to write a report for the organisers of the activity week, telling them how they might improve it for next year.

The organisers have asked you to report on:
- **Whether the week included suitable activities.**
- **Whether the information you were given before the week was the right sort of information.**
- **What new skills you learned during the week.**
- **Things that could be improved.**

PLANNING SHEET

This is for very brief notes to help you plan your ideas. Your notes will not be marked.

First, you might want to make a note of your ideas in these tables.

Things that were good	Things that could be improved

Now use your notes to help you plan your report.

Remember to think about:
- How to describe the activities you took part in and the information you were given.
- How to include examples that will help the organisers understand what you are saying.
- How to end your report.

This is one way to start your report:

REPORT ON SUMMER FUN
I attended the Summer Fun course for one week and have reached the following conclusions.

You may decide to start it another way.

You may write your answer here.

....

....

....

....

....

....

....

....

....

....

....

....

....

....

....

....

....

....

....

....

....

....

....

....

....

....

Test 4: Level 6 Extension

Instructions

You will have 60 minutes for this test, including reading the two texts. Plan your timing carefully and use a clock.

Question 7, the last question, carries the most marks and you should allow up to 30 minutes to complete it, including 5 minutes of preparation time. Good handwriting, grammar and punctuation will earn you marks here. Use a separate sheet of lined paper for this question.

Answer all the questions as fully as you can, giving reasons and examples when requested.

Heroes and Heroines

What is a hero? It is one of those words we are inclined to use loosely. We could think of a pop star as a hero, and we often use the word to describe the leading character in an adventure film – the good guy who wins through against fearful odds. But we use the word more precisely when we are referring to someone whose courage and endeavour really give us something to admire; for example, the Red Cross nurse Edith Cavell, who was shot for helping allied prisoners to escape from Belgium during the First World War. Shortly before she was executed she said, 'I realise that patriotism is not enough, I must have no hatred or bitterness towards anyone'.

Edith Cavell was not considered an important person, like some heroes. So we might think of Henry V of England, who won the battle of Agincourt in 1415, with 6000 exhausted troops, against a French army four times as large. Or Mahatma Gandhi, who led a long struggle for Indian independence while refusing to allow any violence to be used by his followers.

Often we only know a few facts about a hero; we do not always get the full story. For example, few people remember that Henry V had thousands of French prisoners killed during the battle. Gandhi led a simple, threadbare life but one of his followers said: 'If only Bapu (Gandhi) knew the cost of setting him up in poverty!'

Alexander the Great of Macedon (fourth century BC), one of the finest war leaders in history, conquered huge territories across the Middle East and as far as India. He spread the benefits of Greek civilisation through his empire and thus in part paved the way for the Roman and Byzantine empires. Yet he razed cities to the ground, slaughtered thousands and put thousands more into slavery. In a drunken fit he murdered one of his trusted commanders – and then trumped up a charge of treachery to excuse himself. He is often referred to as a hero, and indeed performed many heroic actions, but was he a hero with so much innocent blood on his hands?

We will never know the names of many heroes (although their families may know who they are). Think of a mother who, living on her own and with little money, brings up her family and gives them a good start in the world. How about someone who devotes much of their life to caring for a sick relative – perhaps an ageing parent? Do they not show as much, or more, heroism as a great war leader? If you have seen a war-grave cemetery you will have been impressed by the great field of white tombstones recording the names of a countless number of ordinary people who died to ensure that our generation could live in freedom. In Westminster Abbey, and in other countries, there is a tomb of the Unknown Soldier, standing for all the war dead whose names could never be established.

So, what is a hero?

Anthem for Doomed Youth

This poem has summed up for many people the tragedy of the deaths of so many young men in the First World War. Wilfred Owen, who was born in 1893, was awarded the Military Cross for exceptional bravery in the field in October 1918, and was killed by machine-gun fire on 4 November 1918. The war ended just one week later, on 11 November.

What passing-bells for those who die as cattle?
    Only the monstrous anger of the guns.
    Only the stuttering rifles rapid rattle
Can patter out their hasty orisons.
No mockeries for them from prayers or bells,
    Nor any voice of mourning save the choirs,
The shrill, demented choirs of wailing shells;
    And bugles calling for them from sad shires.

What candles may be held to speed them all?
    Not in the hands of boys, but in their eyes
Shall shine the holy glimmers of good-byes.
    The pallor of girls' brows shall be their pall;
Their flowers the tenderness of silent minds,
And each slow dusk a drawing-down of blinds.

Wilfred Owen (1893–1918)

passing-bell	**tolled to remind Christians to pray for a dying person**
orisons	**prayers**
pall	**velvet cloth, sometimes white, laid over a coffin**

Level 6 Test Questions

1. What is the objective of the writer of 'Heroes and Heroines'? What does he want to leave in the reader's mind when they have read it? Illustrate your answer with reference to clues in the text.

....

....

....

....

....

....

2. A thoughtful piece of writing can often be dull. How has the writer tried to make it interesting? Has he succeeded? Give your reasons with reference to the style and content of the text.

....

....

....

....

2 MARKS

3. Why does the writer move from well-known heroes to ordinary people?

....

....

....

3 MARKS

4. Summarise the message of Wilfred Owen's poem.

....

....

....

....

3 MARKS

5. Wilfred Owen has used many of the 'tools' of the poet to gain his effects. Review the text to identify the tools he has used and give examples.

....

....

....

....

3 MARKS

6. Both Heroes and Heroines and Anthem for Doomed Youth are in different ways about heroes and heroines. Use your best judgement to answer the question, 'What is a hero?', which concludes the first text. Use examples from the texts, or your own examples – as you wish.

....

....

....

....

....

16 MARKS

7. Describe your chosen heroine or hero. They can be someone who is well known either today or in history, or someone you know personally – perhaps a friend or a relation. Or you can choose an imaginary person who must nevertheless sound real. Give a balanced picture both of their qualities, their achievements and their shortcomings, and conclude with reasons why you think they deserve the title. You will be judged by the quality of your writing; make it your best work. Use your own paper for your account.

Glossary

Abstract Noun	Name of something we cannot see, e.g. love, hate, anger
Adjective	A word that describes a noun
Adverb	A word that describes a verb, e.g. quickly, slowly
Alliteration	A string of words in a sentence that start with the same sound or letter, e.g. Silly Susan
Apostrophe	A punctuation mark that shows ownership or where a letter is removed, e.g. Susan's hat isn't for sale
Bibliography	List of books that the author used in research
Contents	List of pages included in the book
Conjunction	A word that joins parts of a sentence, e.g. and, because
Direct Speech	Words that are actually spoken
Fiction	Written material that is made-up, not true
Glossary	List of words that might need explaining
Homophone	A word that sounds like another one, but has a different meaning, e.g. through, threw
Index	List of subjects or names found in a book
Indirect Speech	Reporting words that were spoken
Metaphor	Way of describing something, or painting a word picture, by saying something is something else, e.g. It is raining daggers
Non Fiction	Written material that contains facts or information
Noun	Name of something, e.g. cup, lamp
Onomatopoeia	A word that sounds like the thing it is describing, e.g. tinkle
Plot	The story
Pronoun	Replaces a noun, e.g. I, we, she, he, they
Proper Noun	Name of places, people or things that should be written with a capital letter
Scanning	Looking through a text for key words or phrases
Simile	Way of describing something by comparing it to something else. The words 'as' and 'like' are often used in similes, e.g. My love is like a red, red rose
Skimming	Reading through a passage quickly to just get a broad idea of what it is about
Thesaurus	A book containing words with the same or similar meanings
Verb	An action or doing word

Answers and Marking Scheme: Test 1

(Reading)

Note for parents

The object of the Test is to discover how well your child can understand the meaning of the texts, including the meanings that lie beneath the surface. It is not a test of the quality of the English in the answers, the spelling or the neatness. Although you want to encourage your child, it is no service to mark them leniently – the Testers will not be lenient. It will help you if you study carefully the reading texts, the instructions at the beginning and the questions themselves.

The Legend of Theseus and the Minotaur

1. Part bull, part man.
1 mark

2. A bellow.
1 mark

3. Black sails.
1 mark

4. A sword.
1 mark

5. It made him look angry and fierce.
(Sample answer)
1 mark

6. He wanted his father to know as soon as possible that he had been successful and was safe. (Sample answer)
2 marks

7. So that no one who entered could get out, and would eventually meet the Minotaur. (Sample answer)
2 marks

8. He thought he was in love with her.
(Sample answer)
Clue: he was more determined once she had smiled at him.
Clue: he thought about her on his way home.
3 marks

9. King Aegeus → Fierce and furious
   Minotaur → Determined to be brave
   Theseus → Worried
2 marks

10. Because he had told his father that if he returned alive and successful he would have white sails. When his father saw the black sails, he thought Theseus must be dead.
2 marks

11. Labyrinth.
1 mark

12. So that he could find his way back by unwinding it in the Labyrinth, while she held the other end.
2 marks (Sample answer)

13. The Aegean Sea is in the atlas There are pictures of bull-vaulting in Crete. The palace has many rooms, and could have been the Labyrinth.
3 marks

14. Personal answer. Marks are for the quality of reasons. Full marks are earned only if good reasons are properly supported by the text.
3 marks

Sir Galahad

1. Sword (blade) and lance.
1 mark

2. This was the ladies' way of showing their admiration.
1 mark

3. From the purity of his heart.
1 mark

4. My strength is as the strength of ten.
1 mark

5. Shattering, brands, shiver, tide (of combat) stands, showers. (two required)
2 marks

6. Two should be selected from: shattering, crack, clanging.
2 marks

7. Two should be selected from: shattering, shrilleth, shiver, splinter'd spear-shafts, reel and roll.
2 marks

8. Personal answer. Marks are for the quality of reasons. Full marks are earned only for good reasons that are properly supported by the text.
3 marks

Chinese Myths and Legends

1. his head ⟶ cloud and wind
his breath ⟶ thunder
his voice ⟶ mountain
1 mark

2. Insects and other creatures feeding off his body.
1 mark

3. His see-through body.
1 mark

4. Dragons for ceremonials; picture writing.
2 marks

5. He learnt how to make a shelter from the birds, and then used this to make a more convenient house on the ground.
2 marks

6. He had a dragon's body; his counsellors were dragons.
1 mark

7. Five should be selected from: eating and drinking, making calendars, building houses, dancing, cooking, agriculture, silk weaving, musical instruments, ploughing, writing, medicine.
2 marks

8. Brush and ink.
1 mark

9. Personal answer. Marks are for the quality of reasons. Full marks are earned only for good reasons that are properly supported by the text. Judgement should be made from the ancient Chinese point of view, not because we now think we know better.
3 marks

Answers and Marking Scheme: Tests 2 & 3
(Spelling and Handwriting)

TEST 2: SPELLING TEST

Michael loves playing with his younger cousins, Sam and Luke, but he always gets into trouble. Last year Michael's mother took the three boys on a special day out to a safari park. As usual, the day started well but it wasn't long before the younger boys began to be naughty.

Sam and Luke threw their ice-cream wrappers over the fence, into the giraffe's enclosure. Michael knew it was a bad thing to do, so when his mother's back was turned he climbed over the fence to retrieve the wrappers. The keeper saw Michael standing next to the giraffe. He was furious.

No one was interested in Michael's excuse and the other boys just stood behind a tree, giggling. The keeper suggested Michael be punished for his behaviour and his mother agreed. Poor Michael spent the rest of the day shovelling piles of muck out of an empty antelope cage. Sam and Luke, meanwhile, got to see all the animals.

The following week Luke and Sam's mother offered to take Michael to the cinema. Needless to say, Michael refused. He decided it would be much safer to stay at home and watch television on his own.

Marking the Spelling Test

Number of correct words	Spelling test mark
1–2	1
3–4	2
5–6	3
7–8	4
9–10	5
11–12	6
13–14	7
15–16	8
17–18	9
19–20	10

TEST 2: HANDWRITING TEST

1 mark
Handwriting is legible but inconsistent in size and spacing.
2 marks
Shape and orientation of letters mostly correct, generally of right size and words properly spaced.
3 marks
Letters are partially joined and consistent and regular in size and spacing.
4 marks
Joined writing that is legible with correct ascenders and descenders that are parallel.
5 marks
Handwriting is fluent, joined and legible, showing confident use of style.

TEST 3: WRITING (MARKING SCHEME)

The SATs examiners are given very clear guidelines to help them award marks fairly in the Writing Test. A brief outline is given here.

The children's writing should be assessed with reference to two broad categories:

PURPOSE AND ORGANISATION
Examiners are looking for writing with a clear structure; a beginning, middle and end. They award marks for following the format given correctly (e.g. formal letter, report, story etc.). In imaginative stories examiners look for accurate use of dialogue, new settings, good character descriptions. High marks are given for engaging and sustaining the reader's attention and developing a theme and a plot.

GRAMMAR (SUB-DIVIDED INTO STYLE AND PUNCTUATION)
Examiners are looking for the correct use of sentences and punctuation. Higher marks are awarded to scripts that show a variety of punctuation that is used to show humour or prevent misinterpretation. Examiners look for an interesting style that uses a variety of simple and complex sentences, the appropriate use of language for the format, e.g. standard English or dialect. Well-chosen phrases and attempts to use adventurous vocabulary are also rewarded.

Spelling and handwriting are not assessed in this paper.

Up to 21 marks may be awarded for 'purpose and organisation' and this is equivalent to High Level 5.

Up to 7 marks may be awarded for style and up to 7 marks may be awarded for punctuation. This is equivalent to High Level 5.

Evaluation and Marking Scheme: Tests 2,3 & 4

(Level 6 Extension)

MARKS

This Test is not primarily concerned with right or wrong answers; it is designed to judge your child's ability to interpret and reflect on the texts, and your marking should be based on this.

1. The writer is proposing a question to the reader and uses examples to demonstrate the issues. The identical opening and closing question is a clue, and this is supported by discussing different kinds of heroes and raising the issue of whether a hero needs to be virtuous as well as successful.
3 marks

2. The answer should note that the first sentence both draws the reader in and sets the mood. The interest level is kept high by concrete illustrations, challenging the idea that heroes have to be virtuous, asking the reader questions and extending the types of heroes in an unexpected way.
3 marks

3. In showing that heroism and fame are not the same thing the reader is involved personally. People he or she knows may be heroes; even the reader, by implication, may be called to be a hero. (Sample answer)
2 marks

4. The first part of the poem describes how the slaughter of soldiers is not marked by a bell but by guns, shells and bugles from home. Prayers and bells would be a mockery. It asks how these deaths will be marked. The answer is that it is in the eyes of the dying and the sorrowing of family and friends, which will continue. (Sample answer)
2 marks

5. Two-verse structure showing question and answer.
Use of simile, e.g. as cattle
Use of metaphor, e.g. anger of the guns, stuttering rifles, choirs of wailing shells

Use of 'sounding' words (onomatopoeia), e.g. stuttering, rattle
Use of alliteration, e.g. rifles rapid rattle
Suiting words to feeling, e.g. last line using slow, sad words
Metre and rhyme
3 marks

6. The answer should show awareness that heroism comes in many forms and should discuss whether being virtuous or even successful is a necessary quality. Agreement with the marker's view is not important; quality of evidence for the view taken is.
3 marks

7. This question carries high marks which are not easily earned. The answer should be interesting to read and should show awareness of issues raised by the text; the character described should come across as a plausible person. The reasons why, on balance perhaps, hero status is given should be well argued.

Other factors which will earn or lose marks are:
* good lead in to the piece and good conclusion clear structure
* appropriate variety of sentence and paragraph length
* choice of lively but not affected vocabulary
* appropriate use of literary tools (see question 5, above)
* right level of formality of language
* variety of punctuation properly used
* quality of handwriting and neat corrections
* spelling
16 marks

Total marks = 32

Answers: Revision Section Questions

Page 6
Most people feel nervous, although it usually gets better with practice. Butterflies in the tummy are Nature's way of preparing you for the effort.

Page 7
1. The author uses punctuation, which is why good punctuation in your own writing is important.
2. The other person's. Only when you have listened to them is it time for your point of view.

Page 9
1. Phil was brave because he overcame his fear at the entrance and stood his ground at the end.
2. The author wanted a pause before 'and the moaning' to give dramatic effect to finish the story on a note of terror.

Page 10
1. So that you want to know what happened next, which makes you keen to read the next chapter.
2. Phil. We know because the author has just mentioned Phil, and because the response comes from Meg.

Page 11
1. To show how nervous he was and to show Meg's unselfishness.
2. Replied, exclaimed, declared, remarked.

Page 12
She clutched Phil's arm for comfort. She tried to pull Phil back. She escaped from the cave without waiting for him.

Page 13
Meg and Phil go into a deep, scary cave in a mountain. It's pitch black but, when they go round the corner, a torch beam lights up a ghostly green head. It seems to say 'Beware'. Meg flees, but Phil stays. His torch goes out. What is going to happen next? (Sample answer)

Page 14
1. A list of difficult words in a book that the reader may not be expected to know.
2. A book which gives you alternative or similar words to help you find the exact one you want.

Page 15
1. The Contents gives you the main chapter or subject headings; the Index allows you to look up items or names in the book.
2. The Contents comes at the beginning; the Index comes at the end.

Page 16
The future tense.

Page 17
Mary = noun
Touched = verb
Her = pronoun
Quickly = adverb
On = preposition
Her = adjective
Hand = noun

Page 18
1. C
2. Clatter

Page 19
Check if the poem has three lines of five, seven and five syllables. If it has obeyed the rules, you've done it properly.

Page 20
Bad temper, long greasy hair, never smiles. (Sample answer)

Page 21
He rushed up to the giant. 'I'll knock you down!' he shouted. (Sample answer)

Page 22
There are approximately 18 mistakes, depending on how detailed you wish to be.

When they found the entrance to the cave, Meg and Phil looked inside. It was big and dark.

Phil shivered and said 'Do you think we ought to go in?'

'Don't be silly, Phil,' said Meg. We've finally got here and we can't stop now.'

They switched on their torches, then, holding hands, they went inside. In the dark it felt cold and miserable, and they shivered.

Page 23
'It's raining again.' Tracey moaned.

Her mother said 'Cheer up, Tracy!'

'How can I, when it rains all the time?' Tracey asked.

Page 24
There are many alternatives, e.g. attractive, pleasant, friendly.

Page 25
You need someone else to read your 'hook' and let you know if they think you've succeeded.

Page 27
You need someone else to read your 'hook' and let you know if they think you've succeeded.

Page 28
Mum took the food over to the baby, and fed it. She also took a beaker, a bib and a spoon.

Page 29
1. Ice cream, trifles, cakes, and bread and butter.
2. The first is correct. The second suggests that all astronauts are stupid.

Page 30
It's the children's break, so the dog can have its walk.

Page 31
Can't, won't, shan't, I'll, they're, they'll, didn't, doesn't, it'll, couldn't, etc.

Page 32
I'm writing this story carefully. It's about a weird friend called Keith, who is deceitful and not a success at school.

Page 33
cargoes, loaves, stories, volcanoes, men, eyes, handkerchiefs, mice, calypsos, wives, O'Reillys.

Page 35
Ask an adult to check this for you.

Page 36
Your computers are good quality but I find them rather slow. (Sample answer)

Page 37
Sample answer

Beemer Toys
East Beemer
RG21 2DZ

Miss Mabel Pecksniff

30 November 2002
27 Gringe Road
London
SW19 4LP

Dear Miss Pecksniff,

Re. Your order no. 67A4320 - The Witches of Wimbledon Game

Thank you for your letter of 23 November.

I apologise for sending you the incorrect version of this game. The version that will work with Doors 95 has been despatched, and should be with you shortly.

Please write to me again if you have any further difficulties.

Yours sincerely,

Henry Woggins
Sales Manager